ULSTER WAR MEMORIALS

FROM HISTORY HUB ULSTER

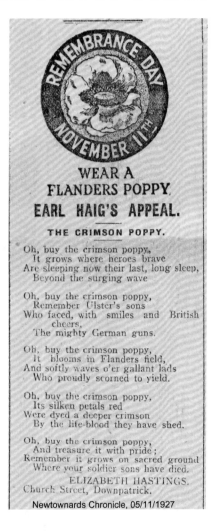

REMEMBRANCE DAY
NOVEMBER 11TH

WEAR A FLANDERS POPPY.

EARL HAIG'S APPEAL.

THE CRIMSON POPPY.

Oh, buy the crimson poppy,
  It grows where heroes brave
Are sleeping now their last, long sleep,
  Beyond the surging wave

Oh, buy the crimson poppy,
  Remember Ulster's sons
Who faced, with smiles and British
    cheers,
  The mighty German guns.

Oh, buy the crimson poppy,
  It blooms in Flanders field,
And softly waves o'er gallant lads
  Who proudly scorned to yield.

Oh, buy the crimson poppy,
  Its silken petals red
Were dyed a deeper crimson
  By the life-blood they have shed.

Oh, buy the crimson poppy,
  And treasure it with pride;
Remember it grows on sacred ground
  Where your soldier sons have died.
      ELIZABETH HASTINGS.
Church Street, Downpatrick.

Newtownards Chronicle, 05/11/1927

A PERSONAL SELECTION

BY NIGEL HENDERSON

HistoryHubUlster

Charity Registration Number: NIC106993

Contact us:
www.historyhubulster.co.uk
research@historyhubulster.co.uk
www.facebook.com/HistoryHubUlster/
@HistoryUlster

Published 2018 by History Hub Ulster and Nigel Henderson

First Edition

First Impression

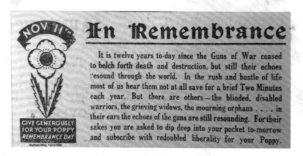

In Remembrance

NOV 11th

It is twelve years to-day since the Guns of War ceased to belch forth death and destruction, but still their echoes resound through the world. In the rush and bustle of life most of us hear them not at all save for a brief Two Minutes each year. But there are others—the blinded, disabled warriors, the grieving widows, the mourning orphans . . . . in their ears the echoes of the guns are still resounding. For their sakes you are asked to dip deep into your pocket to-morrow and subscribe with redoubled liberality for your Poppy.

GIVE GENEROUSLY FOR YOUR POPPY REMEMBRANCE DAY

Designed by April Sky Design, Newtownards
Tel: 028 9182 7195
Web: www.aprilsky.co.uk

Printed by W&G Baird Limited, Antrim

ISBN 978-1-9996588-0-9

Front cover: **Bangor War Memorial**
Designed by Thomas Eyre Macklin of Newcastle-upon-Tyne and constructed by Purdy & Millard of Belfast.
The memorial was unveiled on 24th May 1927 by His Grace The Duke of Abercorn,
Governor of Northern Ireland, and was dedicated by the Right Reverend Charles Thornton Primrose Grierson,
Lord Bishop of Down and Connor and Dromore.

Contents

Preface

I first began to take an interest in war memorials whilst researching the employees of the Belfast Banking Company and the Northern Banking Company who gave their lives in the Great War. In addition to brass tablets listing those who served and the fatalities, both banks produced a series of studio portraits of the men. Currently, the brass tablets and portraits are located in the Head Office building of Northern Bank now Danske Bank. They are displayed in the basement and only accessible to the general public on request. In his book marking the centenary of the Northern Banking Company, Edwin Darley Hill includes a chapter on the Great War which also records the names of seven bank officials who enlisted but were rejected for military service.

One day, whilst having coffee in Flame restaurant on Howard Street, I noticed a plaque and, being curious, I went over to have a look. It transpired to be a commemoration of the laying of the foundation stone for the Presbyterian War Memorial Hostel in 1923. The stone had been covered over at some stage in the past, probably when the Skandia restaurant occupied the space, and had been uncovered during renovations by the current owners. They decided to retain the stone as part of the fabric and history of the building.

This gave me an interest in war memorials that have been hidden, lost, or destroyed over time. More recently, I identified that the war memorial tablet from Elmwood Presbyterian Church in Belfast, which closed in the early 1970s, was held in a store room in Elmwood Presbyterian Church in Lisburn.

I was also involved in a radio interview about the Midland Railway War Memorial which is currently located in the staff car park at the Northern Ireland Railways Yard on York Road in Belfast. It is my hope that the memorials for the men from the three local railway companies will be brought together in one location in Weaver's Cross, the new Belfast Transport Hub.

The back cover of our book features an intriguing form of commemoration – the Belfast Peace Tree which was planted in Woodvale Park in 1919. In 2015, it won the Woodland Trust's Northern Ireland Tree of the Year competition and represented the Province in the European Tree of the Year 2016 competition. Peace Trees were also planted outside the Lisburn Workhouse (on the site of the Lagan Valley Hospital) in February 1920. Whilst the Peace Tree in Woodvale Park thrives, the Peace Trees in Lisburn are no longer there.

During the research phase, the Ulster War Memorials website (maintained by Ken Switzer) and the UK War Memorials Register (maintained by the Imperial War Museum) and local newspapers were consulted. History Hub Ulster (HHU) thanks Philip Orr for writing the foreword for this book and Richard Doherty for reviewing the book and providing editorial comments. HHU also acknowledges the assistance received from Ballymoney Museum, Cavan County Museum, Donegal County Museum, Monaghan County Museum, Chris Hunter (Cookstown), John McCormick (Belfast), and John Stewart (Carrickfergus). Additional photographs were provided by Mark Walmsley (Ulster's War Graves website) and Michael Nugent (WW1 Research Ireland).

History Hub Ulster is pleased to publish this book which highlights war memorials with unusual aspects or are not accessible to the public or whose location is not known. History Hub Ulster wish to thank the Esme Mitchell Trust and the Northern Ireland War Memorial for their generous contributions towards the publication of this book.

Gavin Bamford
Chair, History Hub Ulster

Foreword

When the Great War engulfed Britain and Ireland in 1914, casualties swiftly mounted. The Government faced the challenge of handling war-time mourning and commemoration on a hitherto unknown scale. Vast military cemeteries in France, Flanders and elsewhere began to be the norm. In 1915, General Macready, Adjutant General of the BEF, established a Graves Registration Commission which, in February 1916, became the Directorate of Graves Registration and Enquiries. Graves Registration Units were established to record burials and the locations of cemeteries. Macready's order formalised the work of Fabian Ware whose Red Cross unit had begun collecting information on British dead and where they were buried - usually in scattered informal plots - since September 1914. This remarkable overseas commemorative project, which began in war-time, was successfully completed in the post-war decades

However, the decision to inter the dead and remember the missing where they fell – or close by – contributed to a powerful sense of dislocation in the grieving process for relatives, friends and communities at home. No funeral service was possible, there was no wake to attend and there could be no regular visit to a hallowed plot in a cemetery close to home. This absence of the rituals of grieving was especially acute in an Ireland where such ceremonies were a key part of the culture and where many tens of thousands of young men had perished in the space of four and a half years. Most of them came from tight-knit local communities, which intensified the shock and sorrow.

As a result, both during and after the Great War, a remarkable and diverse array of memorials was created in Ireland, as indeed happened across these islands. These local memorials often located grief and commemoration in tangible, meaningful ways within civic, sacred or familial spaces. Nigel Henderson's work plays an important role in drawing our attention to the subject, a century later.

One countervailing factor for Ireland was the outbreak of a separatist revolution and the creation by 1922 of an Irish Free State which chose to hide the story of the Irish Great War experience underneath its new post-colonial narrative. Nonetheless, several memorials in 'the south' have survived into the 21st century, with some having been lovingly restored in more recent times. Indeed, the most impressive of all Great War commemorative projects is situated in Dublin. The Islandbridge National War Memorial Gardens were conceived of in the immediate aftermath of the global conflict and built in the following decades of Irish independence, only to fall into neglect before restoration and re-opening in 1988. They act as a dignified monument to all those Irish servicemen who served in both global wars.

Many of the local memorials that were created in the fledging state of Northern Ireland, were the result of work by local families, churches, veterans' groups, sporting bodies and businesses. The British Government was happy to underwrite and shape the world-wide work of the Imperial War Graves Commission and to undertake signature domestic projects like the Tomb of the Unknown Soldier and the Whitehall Cenotaph. However, civic memorials were, by and large, established under the aegis of local urban or rural councils who saw it as their task to enumerate the local dead and to remember them.

Despite problems caused by Northern Ireland's political fractures and by the lack of funds in an inter-war era of poverty and economic downturn, the work went ahead – and Nigel's thorough and revealing account gives the reader an insight into the motivations and practice of those involved in Ulster's own memorialisation process. Most of these projects still survive to this day, though some are long gone.

Devising anything with an aesthetic dimension by committee is difficult due to human variations in taste. With the added freight of personal investment brought to commemoration by the grief of those involved, it is understandable that rows did erupt in local committees over the location, style and expense of local projects. The issue of whether a memorial should have a practical dimension to it was a major talking-point. In an often grim and austere post-war world where many veterans suffered from poor job prospects and ill-health, objections were sometimes raised to expensive statues or obelisks, when money could have been spent on a facility that directly assisted the veteran, through housing, training opportunities or leisure facilities.

The added challenge of gathering the names of those who had served and died in an Ulster which was politically divided must also be borne in mind. Already, by 1919, memorial parades were revealing the potential for contention. Nationalists were unwilling to share in the Peace Day celebrations in August of that year. As Ireland headed for partition, northern Catholics and Nationalists often attached a different meaning to their loved ones' sacrifices. Unionists felt that valour had been rewarded by the security of a sustained British presence in the north of the island. However, for many Nationalists who still yearned for an all-Ireland solution, there was a profound sense that costly service in British Army uniform had been in vain.

Sadly, the names of many Catholic servicemen were withheld from inclusion on plaques and monuments in Northern Ireland, though that certainly was not the case everywhere. Other anomalies and omissions were unavoidable, given the difficulty of deciding who merited inclusion on which memorial. There were many challenges in collecting data in an era that long predated the excellent research facilities now available to us. The re-inclusion of omitted names on some of Ulster's memorials has been one recent benefit coming from the preoccupation with the Great War which has lain at the heart of our current decade of Irish political centenaries.

It is also important to recognise that the generation of men and women who created the memorials in Nigel's account felt differently about the war than we do. Most of them had been through the war, many had served in it and almost everyone had lost someone dear to them. We, on the other hand, look back on the period from an ever more distant viewpoint. We are also deeply aware of the way the bloody events of the Great War and its peace treaties only precipitated further wars, most especially the one that began in 1939. The post-war generation of the 1920s and early 1930s did not, by and large, foresee such horror.

And whereas we seek to recall the dead and 'rescue' them from being forgotten, that earlier generation had no problem remembering. Indeed, they often remembered all too well and too painfully. Many of the earliest gatherings to dedicate war memorials projects were celebratory affairs, in which communities were delighted to be free of wartime privations and on the side of the victors. Their young men had put on a uniform and gone to fight the foe and thankfully that foe had been beaten, albeit at a huge cost. That was a reason to celebrate, albeit with a heavy heart.

Philip Orr
Historian, author and playwright

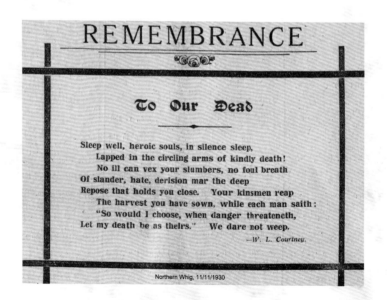

Introduction

To try to cover all war memorials in Ulster – even the civic ones in towns and villages – would be impossible in a publication of this size. This book covers a selection of memorials that are unique in some way and there are sections on memorials that are not immediately accessible to the public and memorials whose location is not known.

In the context of this book, the term "public war memorial" means memorials where responsibility for maintenance was handed over to the relevant civic council. It does not include memorials in public places erected to commemorate members of clubs, associations, societies etc. – a prime example would be the **Strandtown & District Unionist Association War Memorial** on Belmont Road in Belfast.

Whilst most war memorials in churches and organisations come in the form of tablets or plaques and, occasionally, stained glass windows, public or town war memorials take many different forms:

- **Cenotaph** (for example, Belfast, Cookstown, Larne, Newry and the County Tyrone Memorial in Omagh)
- **Obelisk** (for example, Ballynahinch, Kilrea, Ballymena, Tandragee, Kingscourt)
- **Temple** (Lurgan)
- **Victory figure** (for example, Lisburn, Portrush, Londonderry)
- **Soldiers** (for example, County Fermanagh Memorial in Enniskillen, Downpatrick, Dromore and Holywood)
- **Celtic Cross** (for example, Cregagh, Hillsborough)
- **Practical/Functional** (for example, Ballinderry, Castledawson)
- **Clock Tower** (for example, Garvagh, Waringstown)
- **Tablet/Plaque** (for example, Castlewellan, Moneymore)
- **Lychgate** (Crumlin)

In most cases, the public memorials to the fallen of the Great War were erected in the 1920s and 1930s, but some public memorials were erected in the 1950s (e.g. **Rathfriland, Strabane, Sion Mills**) and the 1960s (**Whitehead**). In more recent years, memorials have been erected in several towns (e.g. **Tobermore, Fivemiletown**) whilst memorials are planned for other locations (e.g. **Conlig, Saintfield**). Some of these "new" memorials (e.g. **Dervock. Limavady, Whiteabbey**) replaced memorial halls that had been erected in the inter-war years.

It is interesting that the entire front of St Anne's Cathedral in Belfast was, at the suggestion of Sir Edward Carson, constructed as a monument of victory and a memorial to the men of Ulster who fell during the Great War. A memorial stone was laid by His Grace, the Duke of Abercorn on 2nd June 1925 and a stone marking the completion of the work was dedicated by the Right Reverend Charles Thornton Primrose Grierson on 2nd June 1927.

There are numerous war and regimental memorials in St Anne's Cathedral and a booklet entitled, *The Price of Peace – A Guide to the War Memorials of Belfast Cathedral* is available from the Cathedral Shop.

Female Fatalities

In addition to those women who served in civil roles, women from Ulster served as nurses in a number of different ways, both at home and in theatres of war, with units such as:

- Queen Alexandra's Imperial Military Nursing Service (QAIMNS)
- Territorial Force Nursing Service (TFNS)
- Voluntary Aid Detachment (VAD), an umbrella organisation for the St John of Jerusalem Ambulance Brigade and the British Red Cross
- Ulster Volunteer Force (UVF) Hospitals and
- Scottish Women's Hospitals.

There is, however, some disparity in the commemoration of women who died due to wartime service, both in terms of commemoration on memorials and inclusion in the Commonwealth War Graves Commission database of official war fatalities.

St Anne's Cathedral in Belfast houses a memorial tablet that commemorates the names of 18 Irish nurses who died whilst serving with the QAIMNS or the TFNS during the Great War. The **Irish Nurses War Memorial** tablet was originally installed in the Arbour Hill Garrison Church in Dublin and unveiled on 6th November 1921 by General Sir Cecil Frederick Nevil Macready, the Commander-in-Chief of British Forces in Ireland. On Friday 28th April 1922, the *Northern Whig* carried a report on the Annual Meeting of the Belfast Cathedral Guild during which the Dean of Belfast reported that the Commander-in-Chief of the Forces in Ireland, through the Assistant Chaplain-General, had asked the Guild to receive and place in the Cathedral a tablet erected in the Arbour Hill Garrison Church, Dublin. The Dean said that they were very proud that such a memorial should come to their Cathedral. Whilst several memorials in Ulster have been relocated, the Irish Nurses War Memorial is the one which has been moved furthest from its original location. This is one of only two memorials in Ulster which name the fatalities for a specified corps or regiment – the other is the **North Irish Horse Memorial Window** in Belfast City Hall.

Staff Nurse Elizabeth Harvey Watson (QAIMNS) is also commemorated on the **Dromore War Memorial** in County Down. She was a daughter of Robert H. Watson of Hillsborough Street in Dromore and was 30 years old when she died on 5th November 1918, just a few days before the Armistice. Elizabeth is buried in the Caudry British Cemetery at Nord in France. Sister Rosa McGibbon died of war-related illness on 6th March 1919, aged 32, and is buried in Dougher Roman Catholic Cemetery in Lurgan and is commemorated on the Commonwealth War Graves Commission database but is not commemorated on **Lurgan War Memorial**.

Memorials in several churches and for some clubs and associations commemorate women who died whilst serving with the VAD. The war memorials for the **Strandtown & District Unionist Club** and the nearby **Belmont Presbyterian Church** both commemorate the deaths of Eliza Jane (Ida) Martin, who was serving at a UVF Hospital in Belfast when she died of typhoid fever on 13th June 1917, and Gertrude Annie Taylor, who died of pneumonia whilst serving at 1st London General Hospital in Camberwell on 12th December 1916. The war memorial for the **Cliftonville Cricket and Lawn Tennis Club** commemorates Winifred Elizabeth du Mesney Atkinson who died of appendicitis whilst serving at the Waverley Abbey Military Hospital in Surrey on 14th February 1917. Her name is also commemorated on the **Belfast Royal Academy War Memorial**. These three VAD nurses are buried in Belfast City Cemetery.

However, to the best of my knowledge, only two public memorials in Ulster commemorate VAD fatalities. The **Londonderry War Memorial** commemorates Nurse Laura Marion Gailey, who died of pneumonia at the age of 26 on 24th March 1917 whilst serving in the 1st Western General Hospital in Liverpool. She is buried in the Liverpool (Kirkdale) Cemetery. The **Crumlin War Memorial** commemorates Lizzie Neill Morrison who died of influenza on 2nd July 1918 (more on Lizzie Morrison later).

Of the VAD fatalities named above, Elizabeth Harvey Watson, Laura Marion Gailey and Gertrude Annie Taylor are commemorated as war fatalities by the Commonwealth War Graves Commission, but Ida Martin and Lizzie Neill Morrison are not.

The **Aghadowey War Memorial** commemorates Nurse Annie Kelly Shirley who enlisted with the United States Army Nursing Corps and died of pneumonia on 27th November 1918 at the Military Hospital in Fort Sam Houston in San Antonia, Texas.

Practical War Memorials

There can surely be no more useful kind of war memorial than that of providing a community with an institution which will cater, under a single roof, for a variety of much-felt local needs which are unlikely to be supplied in any other way. With the spirit of comradeship which the war has fostered there has come a desire, now very widespread, that every community should possess a building where — free from sectarian, party, political, or class control — the men and women of the district can meet for social, recreative, educational, or utilitarian purposes, and in which the spirit of comradeship and co-operation can be fostered and find full and free expression.

Sir Alfred Davies, Secretary of the Board of Education
(*Londonderry Sentinel, Thursday 9th March 1922*).

The foundation stone for the **Dervock War Memorial Institute** was laid on 16th September 1919 by Captain Samuel Allen MP, formerly 12th Royal Irish Rifles. The building was erected on land donated by Captain C J McCartney of Lissanoure and was located between the Orange Hall and the Post Office on Main Street. The Institute was officially opened in December 1920 by Mrs McCartney. Before the Institute was demolished in the 1980s, the memorial tablets were removed from the hall and placed in protective display cases in the Memorial Garden. This garden also contains a monument with the inscription, *In memory of those who gave their lives for their country in the cause of justice and freedom. We will remember them.* The base records that it was erected by a grateful community in 1988.

The largest war memorial erected in Ulster in the aftermath of the Great War was the **Presbyterian War Memorial Hostel** on the corner of Howard Street and Brunswick Street in Belfast city centre and had a purely practical purpose. The final building, whilst broadly in keeping with the 1920 artist's impression below, had a more austere and utilitarian appearance.

At the June 1919 General Assembly of the Presbyterian Church in Ireland, the Reverend Andrew Frederick Moody presented his report from the Committee appointed to consider the question of providing a war memorial in connection with the Church:

> The form which the memorial should take has engaged the most anxious and careful consideration of the Committee. It is felt that anything in the nature of statuary would be superfluous, and perhaps inappropriate — superfluous because so many bodies were doing that kind of thing, and inappropriate because there ought to be something specifically Christian about a memorial raised by the Church. The Christian Church stood for a definite idea — the idea of service — and in raising a memorial they should look upon it as a divine trust. It was resolved to recommend that the memorial should consist of two residential clubs — one for the young men, and the other for the young women — because if it were going to be a utilitarian memorial, they must naturally think, first, of those who had served and suffered in the war, and, second, of the class to which they belonged.

In March 1920, the Presbyterian Church in Ireland launched an appeal for subscriptions for the proposed building, which would include 250 individual bedrooms along with a spacious dining hall, lounges, etc. at an estimated cost of £76,000 (£20,000 of which had already been promised or paid). The subscription scheme allowed for "In Memoriam" Rooms, whereby a donation of £100 would entitle a subscriber to furnish a room and have it inscribed in memory of a friend or a relative who had fallen in war service.

The building was designed by Young & Mackenzie, a leading firm of Belfast architects. The contracts to prepare the foundations and to build the superstructure were awarded to two Belfast companies - W J Campbell & Sons of Ravenhill Road and F B McKee of Shore Road. The Admiral of the Fleet, The Earl Beatty, laid the foundation stone on 23rd May 1923. This event was commemorated in a tablet embedded in a wall in the hostel's Dining Room, beneath a smaller tablet which commemorated the opening of the building on 9th June 1926.

The official opening of the building, which had cost £86,000 (approximately £4.8 million in today's terms) to build and equip was performed by Mrs Sara Workman, wife of Mr Frank Workman, the founder of the Workman Clark shipyard. They had lost their only son, Lieutenant Edward Workman MC of the Royal Irish Rifles, who died of wounds on 26th January 1916, aged 29. He was buried in the Etaples Military Cemetery in France and is commemorated on a beautifully engraved Celtic Cross in Belfast City Cemetery, occupying a prominent position overlooking the city and angled to face the shipyards of Belfast.

Although the PRESBYTERIAN WAR MEMORIAL lettering on the face of the building was removed when the building was sold in the 1990s, a shadow of the letters remains visible.

Limavady War Memorial Institute

The Limavady War Memorial Committee obtained "Bridge House" at the western end of Catherine Street from Major Alexander Boyle and converted it into recreation rooms and a free library. The Institute was opened on Thursday 2nd March 1922 by Major General Sir Oliver Nugent and had over one thousand volumes in the library by January 1923. On Thursday 16th October 1924, the Roll of Honour panels listing the men from the district who had served and died in the Great War were unveiled by Major H H F McDonald Tyler

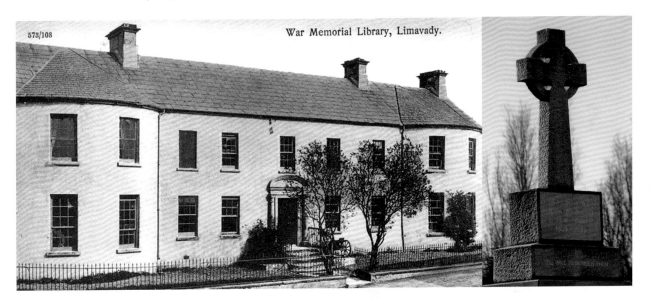

In 1972, the **Limavady War Memorial Institute** was badly damaged in a bomb attack and the building was replaced by the current United Services Club. The Roll of Honour panels were moved to the Green Lane Museum in the Roe Valley Country Park. The current **Limavady War Memorial** takes the form of a Celtic Cross.

Ballinderry War Memorial Hall

On Saturday 5th July 1924, Mr Alfred Sefton laid the foundation stone for the Ballinderry War Memorial Hall in the presence of Sir Crawford and Lady McCullough. The commodious two-storey building, designed without charge by Mr Robert Gilman of Belfast, could accommodate 300 people and contained two auditoria for public functions as well as committee rooms in which fraternal lodges and other organisations could meet.

The building was formally opened on Friday 7th November 1924 by Sir Robert Baird DL in a ceremony over which Mr John Milne Barbour presided. Sir Robert was welcomed by Mr Barbour with the following words, *After the terrible tragedy of the war, it was only right to appreciate the memory of the sacrifices made. It was a happy thought to commemorate them in that way. The hall would serve many useful purposes and would remind them continually of the heroism of the men of their district.*

In his address, Sir Robert Baird commented, *I know the high character Ballinderry, along with its neighbouring districts — Glenavy, Killultagh, Aghalee, Moira, Soldierstown — had always enjoyed for intense loyalty and sound patriotism. The response was not alone on the part of the men who went to the front and did their bit bravely and well, but also on the part of their mothers and fathers, wives, and sweethearts who so far from holding back those they loved so dearly, encouraged them to go out and do their duty. In the splendid Ulster Division and other ranks, on sea and land, the young men of Ballinderry maintained the best traditions of their countryside.*

The *Belfast News-Letter* reported that Sir Robert congratulated the committee upon the form of their memorial, saying that, *the handsome and thoroughly equipped hall would be of practical use to the living for many generations to come, and be a fitting monument, so long as one stone should stand upon another, to those in whose honour it had been erected.*

The Ballinderry War Memorial Hall in County Antrim is still used for community events, although the building is in need of repair.

Belfast

The first cenotaph memorials were temporary in nature and were erected in various locations in Ulster – including Belfast, Kilkeel and Lisburn – in time for the Peace/Victory parades in the autumn of 1919. There are several newspaper photographs of the temporary cenotaph in Belfast. A painting of it by William Gibbes Mackenzie is on display in the Lord Mayor's Corridor in Belfast City Hall.

The **1919 Belfast Cenotaph** was located at the corner of Donegall Square North and Donegall Square East and was the focus for wreath-laying after the Peace Parade on Saturday 9th August 1919. This cenotaph was removed on 19th August 1919.

Belfast Telegraph, August 1919

THE CENOTAPH AT THE CORNER OF DONEGALL SQUARE EAST AND CHICHESTER STREET ERECTED TO THE MEMORY OF ULSTER'S GLORIOUS DEAD. OUR PICTURE SHOWS THE WREATHS PLACED AT THE FOOT OF THE MONUMENT.

THE CENOTAPH AFTER THE WREATHS HAD BEEN PLACED ON IT.

Northern Whig, November 1925

("Northern Whig" Photograph.)

During the 1920s, local newspapers referred to the laying of wreaths during Somme Commemorations and Armistice Day services at a "cenotaph" in the grounds of Belfast City Hall. However, this structure was, in reality, a stepped platform standing approximately three feet high and cannot really be considered to be a "cenotaph".

In 1923, Belfast City Council initiated a public subscription to construct a memorial and a site on the western side of the City Hall was granted by the council in October 1923. However, the call for tenders and designs for a Belfast War Memorial was not advertised until January 1925. Sir Alfred Brumwell Thomas was awarded the contract to design the War Memorial and Garden of Remembrance and the 1924 blueprint (PRONI Reference: LA/7/8/JB/2/20) had the colonnade in its current location but the Cenotaph was to be located in the middle of the garden, along with a Royal Irish Rifles memorial and the Dufferin Memorial. Sir Alfred Brumwell Thomas resigned before the completion of the project and a local firm of architects, Young & Mackenzie, was engaged to complete the project. The Building Contract was issued to W J Campbell & Son and the stone-carving was executed by Purdy & Millard, both being Belfast companies. The **Belfast War Memorial** was unveiled by Viscount Field Marshal Allenby on 11th November 1929 and the service of dedication involved the Right Reverend Charles

THE GARDEN OF REMEMBRANCE.—THE CENOTAPH AND COLONNADE IN THE GARDEN OF REMEMBRANCE AT THE BELFAST CITY HALL.

Northern Whig, 31/03/1928

Northern Whig, 01/10/1927

Thornton Primrose Grierson DD, Lord Bishop of Down & Connor, and the Right Reverend Doctor John Lowe Morrow, Moderator of the General Assembly of the Presbyterian Church in Ireland. However, it is not generally known that the cenotaph was to be topped with a recumbent lion – in October 1927, the *Northern Whig* published photographs of an alabaster model of the lion on the memorial.

In the aftermath of the Great War, the **Irish Sailors' and Soldiers' Land Trust Fund** built houses for ex-servicemen in several locations, including Ypres Park in Whiteabbey, Kemmilhill in Randalstown, Cleenish Island in County Fermanagh, Empire Street in Dungannon and Messines Park in Londonderry (the latter being the only street in Londonderry to suffer fatalities during the German air raids on 15th/16th April 1941).

The largest of the ex-servicemen developments was built on the outskirts of Belfast and became known as the "**Cregagh Colony**", as the houses were surrounded by green fields and were near the terminus of the Cregagh tram line. These houses were nearing completion in April 1925 and the street names all reflected battles or engagements on the Western Front that involved the 36th (Ulster) Division – Picardy Avenue, Bapume Avenue, Thiepval Avenue, Hamel Drive, Albert Drive and Somme Drive.

Rifleman ROBERT HALDANE, Royal Irish Rifles, 162 Templemore Street, Belfast, killed in action. (Photo: Abernethy.)

On 10th November 1929, the **Cregagh War Memorial**, in the form of a Celtic Cross, was unveiled at the junction of Picardy Avenue, Bapume Avenue and Thiepval Avenue by the Right Honourable John Miller Andrews DL MP (whose younger brother, Thomas, Managing Director of Harland & Wolff, perished in the sinking of RMS Titanic). The memorial is dedicated to the men of Cregagh and District but does not have any names recorded.

Master Robert Haldane of Templemore Street laid the Boys' Brigade wreath. He was wearing the three service medals awarded to his father, Rifleman Robert Haldane (8th Battalion, Royal Irish Rifles), who had been killed in action on 2nd July 1916, leaving a widow, Jessie, and seven children, Robert being the youngest.

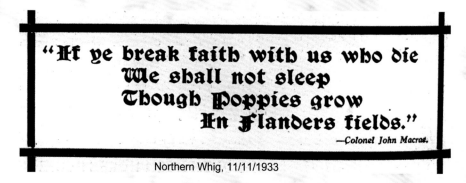

"If ye break faith with us who die
We shall not sleep
Though poppies grow
In Flanders fields."
—Colonel John Macrae.

Northern Whig, 11/11/1933

County Antrim

The **County Antrim War Memorial** at Knockagh, which was designed by Henry Seaver, a Belfast

civil engineer and architect, takes the form of an obelisk and is precisely half the size of the Wellington Monument in Dublin. One of Henry Seaver's sons, Captain Charles Seaver, 8th Battalion Royal Inniskilling Fusiliers, died of wounds on 3rd October 1916 at the age of 22. He is buried in the St Sever Cemetery in Rouen and is commemorated on the Roll of Honour for Malone Golf Club. The memorial looks out over Belfast Lough and is, at 935 feet above sea level, the highest elevated war memorial in Ulster. It is also, at 110 feet, the tallest war memorial in Ulster (although, as mentioned earlier, it was not the *largest* war memorial constructed in Ulster to commemorate the Great War).

On 17th October 1919, the *Belfast News-Letter* reported that, *The general scheme for a permanent War Memorial has been approved of at a meeting of the leading residents in the County. Whilst local memorials will appeal to many, it has been decided, in accordance with the strong opinion expressed throughout the County, that this memorial should take the form of an Obelisk, which will remain for all time a grateful tribute to those from County Antrim who laid down their lives for their King and Country, and whose names will be permanently recorded thereon.*

At the end of September 1922, the *Belfast News-Letter* published a representation of the memorial which, in addition to depicting panels on the base, shows that the names of campaigns and battles were to feature on the faces of the obelisk. The foundation stone was laid by the Countess of Antrim on 7th October 1922 and the construction was largely completed by the end of 1925. In 1932, the LMS-NCC Omnibus Services were providing day trips to the monument. Newspaper reports in 1934 indicate that there was no dedicatory inscription or names on the memorial and, in 1936, responsibility for the completion of the memorial transferred to Antrim County Council. A bequest of £2,500 from Mr Henry Barton of "The Bush" in South Antrim, Honorary Secretary of the County Antrim War Memorial Committee from 1919 until his death in 1934, was used to complete the memorial. The dedicatory panel includes these lines:

> *Nobly you fought, your knightly valour proved,*
> *Your memory hallowed in the land you loved.*

There is no record of the memorial being officially unveiled and, although the dedication and inscription are now engraved in the memorial's stonework, the original lettering (probably made of lead) had been fixed to the memorial. In February 1937, local newspapers reported that the memorial had been vandalised by hooligans, who had prised 21 letters off the memorial.

In Ballymoney, a public meeting was held in the Town Hall in February 1919 and a war memorial committee was established. In February 1920, the *Belfast News-Letter* reported that a public meeting had agreed to the erection of an Irish Round Tower as a suitable memorial, with a plaque naming the fatalities from the district. This scheme did not come to fruition and it was not until after the Second World War that a simple plaque was erected at the British Legion Hall. The names of the fallen from the Great War were not established until Robert Thompson published Ballymoney Heroes 1914-1918 in 1999. The war memorial area outside the Royal British Legion Hall now includes a set of panels naming the local fatalities from both world wars and a sentinel soldier (made by Beltane Studios of Peebles) stands outside the hall. The statue was unveiled on 1st November 2014 by Bill Kennedy, Mayor of Ballymoney.

Whilst most war memorials in towns commemorate the fallen from both the urban and rural councils of the day, the **Larne War Memorial** only commemorates the fallen from the Larne *Urban*

District Council area. The memorial is a cenotaph, albeit with the addition of a soldier (a sergeant) and a sailor. It is one of only two town memorials in Ulster to have this feature and it is the only war memorial in Ulster to depict a soldier and sailor holding hands! The memorial is also unique as a German pickelhaube helmet lies at the feet of the soldier.

The corners of the cenotaph feature lions' heads – a sailing ship and the town's motto **Falce Marique Potens** (Powerful with the sickle and on the sea) are engraved between the lions' heads on the front and rear faces whilst the words **France** and **Belgium** are engraved between the lions' heads on the other two faces. The figures on the war memorial were sculpted by Frederick William Pomeroy of London, whose other works include the pediment of Belfast City Hall, the statue of Brigadier General Nicholson in Lisburn and sculptures for several other local war memorials, including Coleraine and Cookstown.

The **Larne War Memorial** was originally erected outside the Laharna Hotel at the junction of Main Street and the Glenarm Road, and was unveiled by Colonel Robert Chaine Alexander McCalmont DSO on 7th March 1922. The Larne War Memorials Committee had purchased Inver house, the former home of the Barklie family, and the building was handed over to the Larne Branch of the British Legion in March 1922 for use as a club and recreation ground for ex-service men. As early as 1933, the Larne Urban District Council considered relocating the war memorial due to the increasing volume of motor traffic. Despite several traffic accidents at the junction where the war memorial was located, there was local opposition to the suggestion, as demonstrated in a letter in the *Larne Times and Weekly Telegraph* on 20th May 1933 from Beatrice Kirk of the Women's Section of the Larne Branch of the British Legion. The current Garden of Remembrance was bought from Larne and Inver Parish Church in 1973 by Larne Borough Council and developed by Enterprise Ulster, the war memorial being transferred to the park in May 1975.

The **Crumlin War Memorial** is the only one in Ulster to take the form of a lychgate and was originally the entrance to the War Memorial Park. It was unveiled by Viscount Massereene and Ferrard, Lord Lieutenant for County Antrim, on Saturday 8th July 1922. Viscount Massereene served with the North Irish Horse during the war and his wife served with the VAD. The coverage in the *Northern Whig* on Monday 10th July 1922 included this description of the memorial gardens:

> *The park has been laid out near the railway station in Crumlin and covers an area of four and a half acres. A memorial gateway of solid oak, erected near the main entrance contains two tablets, on which are the names of those who fell and also of those who served in the war. The park had been laid out and the gateway erected to the memory of thirty-two good men and true who made the same supreme sacrifice in the late war, to nine men and women who died on service or from the effects of illness and disease contracted on service, and to 164 men who willingly and freely gave their services to their country. The park contains both cricket and football grounds, and tennis courts are being prepared. There is also a playground for the children.*

The **Crumlin War Memorial** is one of only two public memorials in Ulster which commemorate females who died whilst serving with the VAD, the other being the **Londonderry War Memorial**. The tablets for the Great War are in the covered section of the lychgate, whilst corresponding panels for the Second World War have been placed on its outer walls. When the park was replaced by a leisure centre and car park, the lychgate was relocated so that it is adjacent to the car park within a railed-off area. The memorial was rededicated in 2015, when an interpretive panel was also installed.

Belfast Weekly Telegraph, 08/07/1922

The VAD recorded on this memorial is Lizzie Neill Morrison, a daughter of William Morrison and Jane Morrison (nee Neill), who was born on 19th April 1888 near Killead in County Antrim, where the family farmed land. Lizzie's father died of stomach cancer on 3rd July 1889, her mother taking over the running of the farm. In the early 1900s, Lizzie's eldest brother, James, took over the running of the family farm and Lizzie was living with her mother and another brother, Robert Neill Morrison (a bank official), at 396 Lisburn Road. In 1901, another brother, John, was a medical student at Edinburgh University.

Lizzie enlisted with the Scottish Women's Hospitals via the British Committee of the French Red Cross and served as an orderly between August 1916 and May 1917, initially at Lake Ostravo in Salonica and later in Serbia. She contracted malaria whilst in the Balkans and was invalided home. When she had recuperated, she joined the VAD in June 1918 and moved to London, where she lived with her brother, Dr John Morrison. Lizzie contracted influenza and died of pneumonia on 2nd July 1918, aged 30. Tragically, her brother died of influenza on the following day. Lizzie is *not* commemorated as an official war fatality on the Commonwealth War Graves Commission database but is commemorated on the War Memorial tablet in Killead Presbyterian Church and on the Morrison family memorial in the church graveyard.

County Armagh

On Friday 9th January 1925, a meeting was held at the City Hall in Armagh to consider the question of erecting a war memorial for the city of Armagh. The Chairman of the meeting, Senator H B Armstrong, reported that previous proposals put forward in 1922 for a County Armagh War Memorial had not been enthusiastically welcomed and, as memorials were planned for other towns in the county, it seemed strange to many that there was no memorial planned for the capital of the county. At a meeting of subscribers on Monday 16th March 1925, it was decided that a memorial should be erected at the north end of the Mall, opposite the County Courthouse. In July 1925, the Armagh War Memorial Committee purchased Charles Leonard Hartwell's figure "Glory to the Death", which had been exhibited in the Royal Academy, and commissioned him to erect it as a war memorial in Armagh. The **Armagh War Memorial** features a female figure holding palm fronds and a laurel wreath, representing peace with honour. On Friday 3rd December 1926, the memorial was unveiled by the Governor of Northern Ireland, James Albert Edward, the Duke of Abercorn, and was dedicated by the Primate of All Ireland, the Reverend Doctor Charles Frederick D'Arcy.

On Tuesday 21st August 1923, a public meeting in Portadown Town Hall set in motion a process that resulted in the erection of the **Portadown War Memorial**. The ex-servicemen who attended the meeting expressed the view that the memorial, *should take the form of a statue, and not be in any sense utilitarian.*

In January 1925, the Portadown Urban District Council decided that the statue of Colonel Saunderson in front of St Mark's Church should be moved to facilitate the erection of the war memorial. It was reported at council that the family of Colonel Saunderson had expressed honour at the statue being placed beside the war memorial. At this meeting, the design submitted by Henry Charles Fehr of London was accepted and the Belfast firm of Purdy and Millard was engaged to relocate the Saunderson Statue and, it is assumed, the same company was responsible for erecting the war memorial. Charles Fehr was of Swiss heritage and a founding member of the Royal British Society of Sculptors in 1904, later becoming a Fellow of the Society. He was responsible for designing several war memorials, including the ones in Leeds, Colchester and Lisburn (all of which feature statues of winged figures, representing "Victory").

In June 1925, it was decided that the War Memorial and the Saunderson Statue should be placed abreast, separated by a space of about 25 feet, and at a distance of about 40 feet from the eastern (or front) boundary wall of St Mark's Churchyard. The war memorial in Portadown features a winged figure representing victory, with a laurel wreath held in her left hand, alighting on sandbags and gazing down at a wounded soldier, whose helmet has slipped to reveal a bandaged head. Although this precise combination is unique for war memorials within Ulster, the memorial has a further exceptional feature in that a gas mask lies near the feet of the soldier. The soldier, despite his wounds, is still standing and is holding his grounded rifle, which denotes perseverance. The bronze group is approximately 12 feet high and rests on a plinth of Irish granite to which bronze panels recording the names of the fallen from the Portadown district are affixed.

The **Portadown War Memorial** was unveiled by Lieutenant General Sir Travers Clarke, late of 1st Battalion Royal Inniskilling Fusiliers, on 13th November 1925. It was dedicated by the Lord Primate of All Ireland, the Most Reverend Doctor D'Arcy, with prominent clergy from the Presbyterian and Methodist denominations also involved in the service.

There was extensive coverage of the ceremony in the *Portadown Times* on 20th November 1925, which listed the churches, organisations (including the Orange Order and the Ancient Order of Hibernians), commercial companies and individuals who laid wreaths - many of which were dedicated to individual men. The newspaper coverage also listed the names of the fatalities recorded on the memorial by the street or townland where they had lived.

The following poem, dedicated to the fallen of Portadown, was published in a supplement of the *Portadown Times* on 20th November 1925:

They heard their country calling,
    At grips with mighty foe,
Nor paused; - the cost uncounting
    When duty whispered, "Go!"
Our youth at manhood's dawning:
    Our manhood – noble grand;
With one consent responded:
    "We come – our motherland."
They faced the battle's terrors,
    The cannons awful din,
The carnage and the bloodshed,
    Unborne by power within:
And many now lie sleeping,
    With crosses row on row
To mark the spot – while o'er the scene
    The Flanders poppies grow.

And others' bones lie bleaching
    Where rock-strewn Dardanelles
Bears witness to the courage
    That is our race still dwells;
All silently, - all quietly
    All peacefully, - they lie,
Until the great Archangel's trump
    Shall summon to the sky.
For husbands, friends and brothers,
    For sons who'll ne'er return,
We raise this stone of memory,
    We – who are left to mourn:
And should we grow forgetful,
    Their valour fail to prize,
This monument will, silent, speak
    Of their great sacrifice.

County Cavan

The **County Cavan War Memorial Committee** decided to commemorate the county's war dead by erecting and equipping an operating theatre at the County Cavan Infirmary, with the names of the fatalities being recorded on a tablet attached to the building. The *Anglo-Celt* newspaper carries several articles relating to discussions by the Infirmary's management board, but there is no record of the operating theatre being built. The War Memorial Committee's proposal coincided with a major restructuring of hospital services in the Irish Free State, and it is possible that the money raised was used to construct an operating theatre, but not one that was dedicated as a war memorial. In July 1922, the County Cavan War Memorial Committee was wound up with a credit balance of £57.

The congregation of **Virginia Church of Ireland** in County Cavan erected two war memorials – a Celtic Cross in the grounds and a tablet within the church. Both bear the names of the four men from the parish who died in the Great War. The War Memorial Tablet was installed in the church in 1920 and features the insignia of the three regiments to which the men belonged.

The base of the War Memorial Cross features an engraving of a King's Crown within a Victor's Crown of laurel leaves, under which the names of the four fatalities are engraved. Below the names the words "Faithful Unto Death" are engraved.

The memorial was unveiled by Major General Sir Oliver Nugent on Sunday 26th August 1923 and the ceremony was reported in the *Irish Times*. In his sermon, the Bishop of Kilmore dealt at some length with the work of the League of Nations and said that:

> *the most fitting memorial to the memory of those four men and the millions of others who had given their lives in the great war, would be an effective League of Nations and International Court of Justice, so that the necessity for war as a means of settling international disputes might be obviated in the future.*

County Donegal

Several memorials commemorating fatalities from the Great War have been erected in County Donegal in recent years – for example, a memorial wall commemorating the men of the Inishowen Peninsula at Fort Dunree (2011) and a memorial in the grounds of St Eunan's Cathedral in Letterkenny (2014). However, the only public memorial erected in the inter-war years in County Donegal was in the village of **Pettigo**, on the border between the counties of Donegal and Fermanagh.

It is not known who designed the memorial or when it was erected, but it is known that it was constructed by John Robinson & Son of York Street in Belfast. The first name on the memorial is that of Captain Norman Leslie of the Rifle Brigade, who is also the first fatality named on the St Salvator Church of Ireland War Memorial on the Castle Leslie Estate in Glaslough, County Monaghan.

Norman Jerome Beauchamp Leslie was the second son of Colonel (later Sir) John Leslie and Leonie Jerome, of Castle Leslie, Glaslough, County Monaghan. His mother was an American and was the sister of Winston Churchill's mother, Jennie. He was educated at Eton and Sandhurst and was commissioned in 1905, joining the Rifle Brigade in October of that year. He was deployed to France on 10th September 1914 with 3rd Battalion (which had been stationed in Cork at the outbreak of the war) and was killed in action on 19th October 1914 by a German sniper while on reconnaissance at Armentières, near Lille. Captain Leslie is buried in the Chapelle-d'Armentières Old Military Cemetery and he was posthumously Mentioned in Despatches by General Sir John French, whose despatch was published in the London Gazette in February 1915.

County Down

The **Banbridge War Memorial** features a pedestal and pillar of Portland stone, topped with a bronze figure of a soldier holding his grounded rifle in his left hand and his helmet in the right hand. The commemorative booklet produced after the dedication of the war memorial includes a photograph of the soldier, with the caption, *Come on the Bann!*

The war memorial is unique within Ulster due to the bronze friezes on each of the four faces of the pillar which, like the soldier, were designed by Frederick William Pomeroy of the Royal Academy.

The friezes feature battle scenes, evoking the horrors of war whilst depicting the self-sacrificing heroism of soldiers in the fighting line, and each frieze has an engraved title. Panel 1 ("Defending The Flag") features a standard bearer with colours aloft whilst an officer is slumped on the ground firing a revolver. They are surrounded by soldiers with rifles raised to defend the colours and their officer. Panel 2 ("The Great Attack 1916") features men preparing for an attack with one soldier viewing the battlefield through binoculars, whilst a machine gunner lays down covering fire. Panel 3 ("In The Trenches") depicts the weariness and loss in battle, the centrepiece being two soldiers struggling with the corpse of a comrade whilst their captain, revolver held loosely, looks on with dejection etched on his features. Panel 4 ("Le Cateau 1914") depicts soldiers engaged in a bitter defence of their trench, whilst on both sides of the foreground downed German soldiers are being despatched and a German on horseback is being pushed over.

The memorial commemorates those who died during the Great War and was unveiled on 11th November 1923 by Colonel Robert David Perceval-Maxwell DSO. After the ceremony, the entourage moved into the Banbridge Free Library where a Roll of Honour commemorating the names of those who served and came home was unveiled by Mrs N D Ferguson, the wife of Captain T D Ferguson MC. The teakwood tablet, which has brass panels, sits on a heavily-moulded pediment bearing the town's crest. It was designed by a Banbridge-born artist, Edith

Sarah Emerson, a teacher at the Metropolitan School of Art in Dublin. The Roll of Honour tablet is currently displayed in the Banbridge Civic Centre.

Not far outside Banbridge lies the townland of Magherally and the war memorial at **Magherally Presbyterian Church** is worthy of particular mention. The obelisk, which stands at the edge of the church grounds, has a dedicatory panel and list of fatalities on the front face and a list of those who served on the reverse face. The side faces feature bronze reliefs, designed by Edith Sarah Emerson, depicting scenes of war on land and at sea.

The conflict on land panel depicts the British Army coming to the rescue of Belgium. In the foreground at the bottom is a German trench with a mortar being fired. In the middle ground, there is a wounded soldier lying on the ground but holding up a standard which a British soldier is reaching out to grasp. Further back, along the side of the marching troops are the figures of a woman and child – the defenceless. There are two broken pillars – symbolising lives cut short – and a fallen pillar. In the background are the ruins of mighty buildings and at the very top there is an aeroplane in one corner and a cross on a hill, the latter symbolising the righteousness of the Allied cause. Around the rim of the panel are these words:

ALL THEY HAD HOPED FOR ALL THEY HAD
THEY GAVE TO SAVE
MANKIND THEMSELVES THEY SCORNED TO SAVE
LEST WE FORGET

The conflict at sea panel depicts a Royal Navy vessel ramming a German submarine to protect a merchant ship, visible in the background. In the bottom corner is a mine, symbolising the dangers faced at sea. In the far background is a rising sun whose rays are dispersing the clouds over the warship, symbolising that the war would herald a brighter future. Around the rim of the panel are these words:

WE HAVE FED OUR SEA FOR A THOUSAND YEARS AND SHE
CALLS US STILL UNFED THOUGH
THERE'S NEVER A WAVE OF ALL HER WAVES BUT MARKS
OUR BRITISH DEAD

The memorial was constructed by the Banbridge and Newry Granite Works and was unveiled on 24th October 1920 by Mrs Crawford of Belfast and dedicated by the Reverend Doctor William James Lowe, Clerk of the General Assembly of the Presbyterian Church in Ireland.

Edith Sarah Emerson was the daughter of James Edmund Emerson, Proprietor of the *Banbridge Chronicle*, and sister of James Edmund Emerson, Proprietor of the Banbridge and Newry Granite Works.

Newtownards has the distinction of having had four war memorials, each made from a different material. In March 1924, the *Newtownards Chronicle* reported that unemployed ex-soldiers of Newtownards took full advantage of a heavy fall of snow to build a memorial to fallen heroes. It featured a pedestal, standing eight or nine feet in height, topped with a snowman, complete with the representation of a rifle, medals, haversack and steel helmet.

Sources: www.ulsterwarmemorials.net; Newtownards Chronicle - 07/07/1928 and 26/05/1934

In 1925, members of the British Legion erected a plywood obelisk in Conway Square in time for the annual Somme Commemoration ceremony. After the Somme service in 1927, members of Newtownards British Legion decided to erect a more permanent memorial and volunteers made a concrete obelisk, modelled on the previous plywood memorial, in the grounds of the Legion Headquarters in Victoria Avenue. Commemoration events were reported as being held at the war memorial at the British Legion Hall as late as 1941.

The **Newtownards and District War Memorial** is located in a park, the land having been donated to the town by the Marquis of Londonderry, at the junction of Castle Street and Church Square. Ironically, as the above montage of images shows, the memorial is in a very similar position to that of the 1924 Snowman Memorial. The memorial, an obelisk made from Mourne granite, was unveiled by the Marquis of Londonderry, Secretary of State for Air, on Saturday 25th May 1934. The front face of the memorial features three engraved reliefs – at the base is the town crest, above the dedicatory panel is a female figure holding out palm fronds (symbolising Peace with Honour) and, at the top, is a composite engraving in which a lion's head, laurel wreath and fasces (symbolising Strength, Victory and Justice) are inter-woven. The memorial was erected by Purdy & Millard of College Square North in Belfast.

Newry was the last major town in Ulster to erect a public memorial to commemorate local fatalities of the Great War. During the inter-war years, Armistice Day commemorations were held beside temporary structures located in Margaret Square and, later, Trevor Hill. In November 1929, the War Memorial Committee had accepted a proposal for a decorated Celtic Cross from Samuel Wilson Reside, a civil engineer from Margaret Square in Newry, but this memorial was never constructed. An alternative design by Samuel Wilson Reside, a cenotaph with a carved wreath in relief on each face, was constructed by McEwen Granite. On 8th September 1939, the *Irish Independent* reported that the planned unveiling of the memorial had been deferred

Weekly Telegraph, November 1929

due to the declaration of war by Prime Minister Chamberlain. The local newspapers reported that the war memorial was to be placed in Trevor Hill but the cenotaph is located in Bank Parade, near Newry Town Hall.

The **Newcastle War Memorial**, which stands outside the Visitors' Centre in Newcastle (formerly the Annesley Arms Hotel), is the only civil memorial from the inter-war years in Ulster that has an animal as the predominant feature.

In August 1923, two German trophy guns were positioned at Blackrock Promenade, where there was also a wooden memorial which many felt was not in keeping with the dignity of a prosperous seaside resort. The annual Armistice Day commemorations were held at this memorial until 1926 and laying wreaths at the trophy guns was part of the annual parade in 1928. In November 1924, a deputation from the local branch of the British Legion attended a meeting of the Newcastle Urban Council to complain that the park in which the trophy guns had been placed was not being maintained by the council and to request co-operation in the erection of a war memorial in the form of an obelisk. On 4th December 1924, a public meeting was held at which three suggestions were put forward – an obelisk on the Blackrock Promenade; conversion of the "islands" into a War Memorial Park; and erection of a Town Hall. On Wednesday 2nd September 1925, a public meeting accepted the recumbent lion design by Lady Mabel Annesley, who undertook to cover the costs of the sculpture. The memorial was to be placed in front of the baths (at a site donated by a Mr McCartney) adjacent to the Annesley Arms Hotel.

The recumbent lion was sculpted in granite by Francis Wiles of Larne and was in place by November 1928, although there is no record of the memorial being unveiled or dedicated. In March 1937, when a deputation from the Newcastle Branch BL requested that the war memorial be floodlit, council officials pointed out that the memorial, *had neither been dedicated to the public nor vested in the local authority.*

The memorial records the names of 25 men from the Newcastle district who fell during the Great War and 17 men who died during the Second World War. The first name on the memorial is that of Francis Annesley, 6th Earl Annesley of Castlewellan, who was the first earl to be killed in the Great War. Francis Annesley was in the Royal Naval Reserve at the outbreak of the war and distinguished himself serving with the Royal Naval Air Service's Armoured Car Division, helping to check the advance of the Germans on Brussels and in the defence of Antwerp. Francis Annesley was last seen alive on 6th November 1914 after leaving Eastchurch in England in a Bristol biplane flown by Flight Lieutenant Beevor, RNAS, bound for France. His death was presumed on 2nd December 1914 by Mr Justice Astbury. The interrogation of two German prisoners had established that the two aviators had been shot down when a German shell had hit the petrol tank of their aircraft and it had fallen in flames near Diksmuide.

County Fermanagh

The **County Fermanagh War Memorial** is situated at the junction of Belmore Street, East Bridge Street and Queen Elizabeth Street in Enniskillen. In June 1920, it was reported in local newspapers that the Fermanagh County War Memorial, for which a sum of £1,600 had been subscribed, would take the form of a brass tablet, inscribed with the names of the fallen, and would be placed in Enniskillen Town Hall. The remainder of the money raised would be given to the Improvement Fund of the County Hospital as a memorial, with a suitable tablet being erected to mark the reason of the gift. In September 1920, a special meeting of the subscribers to the War Memorial Fund rejected this decision as subscribers felt that the money had been collected for a public monument to be erected in a public position in Enniskillen. At this stage, a committee was established to determine the nature and form of the memorial.

The architect for the project was Richard Pierce, and Philip Flannigan sculpted the Sentinel

Courtesy: Inniskillings Museum

Courtesy: Michael Nugent

Soldier that stood on a 20-foot high plinth, which features an engraving of the Inniskillings crest and an interlaced sculpture of a rifle, sabre and laurel wreath at its base. The memorial was unveiled on 25th October 1922 by Viscount FitzAllen of Derwent, Lord Lieutenant of Ireland.

Not only is this the only one of the three "county" memorials to feature the names of the fallen but it was the only public memorial in County Fermanagh to commemorate the Great War. The original memorial was partially replaced following the Enniskillen bombing in 1987, with doves being added to the plinth on which the soldier stands. A section of the original memorial is now on display outside the Royal British Legion Hall in Fivemiletown, County Tyrone.

In 2017, a panel listing the names of local men who died in the Great War was added to the Boer War Memorial in Brookeborough.

County Londonderry

The **Londonderry War Memorial** consists of three separate statues on plinths and was designed by Vernon March of Farnborough in Kent (who also designed the Canadian National War Memorial, "The Response", in Ottawa).

Photograph: Courtesy of Mark Walmsley

Photograph: Courtesy of Mark Walmsley

It was unveiled by Major General Felix Fordall Ready on 23rd June 1927. The central structure is 38 feet and six inches high and features a statue of a winged figure of Victory – the right hand holds aloft a laurel wreath, the left hand holds a drawn but lowered sword and the right foot is crushing a serpent. There is a dedicatory inscription on the front face of the plinth and there are bronze lozenges, on which the fatalities (including VAD Nurse Laura Marion Gailey) are named, at the four corners of the plinth. On Victory's right-hand side, is a statue of a bare-footed sailor *coming hurriedly on deck, pulling on his oilskins as he goes, and having all the atmosphere and spirit of the sailor (Londonderry Sentinel, 25th April 1925).* The name band on the sailor's hat is **HMS Derry**, although there was no ship with this name during the Great War. On Victory's left-hand side, is a statue of a soldier in the act of taking a trench.

As part of the report on the unveiling and dedication of the war memorial, the *Londonderry Sentinel* (25th June 1927) included this poem, entitled *Derry's Own*, by Miss Lily Marcus:

Soldier of ours, You went away In the morning time of life's glad day, When the far-off ranks of War were calling, And the homeland tears for you were falling. Mingling a melody, loved of long, With the unfamiliar battle-song, Valiant and free, you entered the strife, With a thought, perchance, of th' dreams of life, Yet nobly facing the grim attack, But, soldier of ours, you didn't come back! And here in our gardens bloom the flowers, In the soft June peace of this land of ours, The peace we kept through the life you gave! There are flowers, too, on your distant grave, And truer than word of tribute said, Is Memory's wreath of poppies red, And the sweet home-flowers of pensive hue, Fragrant and pure as the thought of you. And now as we place them Beneath your name, Enshrined in this fair, white stone, We are proud that Victory spreads her wings O'er a name of Derry's Own.	Sailor of ours, 'Twas you who passed Out by the way of the ocean vast, That great white gate to the paths of Glory, Where the winds and waves repeat your story. Over the waters they sing it yet, And Mem'ry hears, and cannot forget How safe were the bounds of our Island 'home, Because of you on the war-strewn foam, As you guarded for us the ocean's track, But, sailor of ours, you didn't come back! And th' zephyrs wait in the sunset West, To whisper of how you found your rest, Somewhere unknown, till the shadows flee, But, somewhere in Love's eternity! And we bring you, too, the flowers of June, All hushed in dreams by the wild waves' croon Stealing from over the Summer sea, That you kept so proudly, grandly free. And now as we place them Beneath your name Enshrined in this fair, white stone, We are proud that Victory spreads her wings O'er a name of Derry's Own.	Heroes of ours, Ye nobly won The rest that came when the day was done, The day that crowned you with human splendour, And wrapped you in slumber calm and tender. And there are laurels the flowers among, For you, who passed to the victor-throng By the way of Glory's lifted gates, And here in the homeland Mem'ry waits With comrades of old, who shared with you All, save the Silent, Last Review, Yea, waits where Love on your names looks down, Yet over the cross beholds the crown, As it hears the harp of life, all mute, Finding its chords in the Grand Salute, That rang o'er a Higher Home-bound track To welcome you who didn't come back. And now as we honour Your Silent Roll Enshrined in this fair, white stone, We are proud that Victory spreads her wings O'er the names of Derry's Own.

Whilst the names of six regions in which fighting took place (Belgium, France, Palestine, Mesopotamia, Gallipoli and Italy) are engraved on the **Lurgan War Memorial**, the **Kilrea War Memorial** in County Londonderry is the only memorial within Ulster that is engraved with the names of battles and campaigns of the Great War in which men named on the memorial participated:

- Marne, St Quentin and Egypt;
- Mons, Somme and Gallipoli;
- Aisne, Guillemont and Egypt; and
- Ypres, Messines and Palestine.

The granite obelisk was erected over a well in the Diamond in Kilrea. According to the *Ballymena Weekly Telegraph* (4th July 1925), the area had been, *a source of contention between rival political sections as to whose party emblem should adorn it. Now the Diamond contains an emblem of unity, for the memorial symbolises the part which local men of all grades played in the great struggle of the Empire.* The war memorial was designed by Samuel James McFadden, Civil Engineer and Architect of Queen Street in Coleraine, and notices inviting tenders from contractors were advertised in local newspapers in May 1924. Contractors would be provided with a copy of the drawing and specification on payment of a non-refundable fee of a Guinea. Construction work was underway by the end of that year.

On 1st July 1925, Mrs Dehra Chichester OBE, of Moyola Park in Castledawson, presided over a ceremony in which the Kilrea War Memorial was unveiled by Lady Anderson, Mayoress of Londonderry from 1915 to 1919, who later presided over the unveiling and dedication of the Londonderry War Memorial. Mrs Chichester had been elected as an MP for the Londonderry constituency in the Northern Ireland Parliament in 1921 and represented the constituency until 1929. She was returned unopposed as the MP for the South Londonderry constituency in a 1933 by-election and served until her resignation on 15th June 1960 – she was the longest serving female MP in the history of the Northern Ireland Parliament.

The memorial lists the names of those who died and those who served in the Great War, with a separate panel listing the names of eight local women who served as nurses.

SERVED
NURSES
HILL KATHLEEN A McCAHON MARTHA
KENNEDY JEANNIE McFADDEN KATHLEEN
McCAHON SARA   McILRATH CAROLINE
MICHAEL HESSIE
SCOTT ANNIE B

Some of the names of Great War servicemen appear out of alphabetical sequence, indicating that names had been added to the memorial after its dedication but before the inscription of names for the Second World War.

The **Garvagh War Memorial** is a splendid example of a battlemented clock tower with four illuminated clock faces and inset with three black granite tablets, naming those who served and those who died. The memorial tower was erected on land, adjacent to the demesne and overlooking Main Street, which was donated by Mr Edward Stronge of Garvagh House. The tower, which was designed by Thomas Johnston of Lisachrin, was constructed of black cut stone and is 40 feet high and 9 feet square. The building contractor was Thomas Fleming of Killyvalley and the building

work was executed by three local men - John Lamont, Robert Faith and Hugh Faith. Alexander L Mann, a watchmaker in Garvagh, procured the clock from the Midlands Clock Works in Derby and undertook to keep it in order. Mr J McAfee of Coleraine executed the engravings on the first-tier lintels: FOR KING is engraved on the eastern face above the tablet naming those who died, FOR GOD is engraved on the southern face above a tablet naming some of those who served and FOR COUNTRY is engraved on the northern face above a tablet naming the remainder of those who served, including the names of seven female nurses.

Access to the interior and to the clock mechanism is via a door on the western side. The door's lintel is engraved as follows: T A Johnston, Architect; T T Fleming, Building Contractor; A L Mann, Clock Contractor; and J McAfee, Sculptor. Captain Charles Edmond Sinclair Strong DL of Aghadowey unveiled the memorial on 27th March 1924 and his wife started the clock mechanism.

THE GREAT WAR 1914-1918

The seven named nurses include two young women with the surname McNeary, although no familial connection has been established.

William John McNeary, a baker with premises on Garvagh's Main Street, had married Florence White in Ballywillan Presbyterian Church on 18th July 1884 and their fourth child, Florence, was born in Garvagh on 15th April 1891. Florence served with the VAD at the Royal Salop Infirmary in Shrewsbury from April 1916 and was still serving in March 1919.

Thomas Alexander McNeary, a woollens and drapery merchant with premises on Garvagh's Main Street, had married Emily Rebecca McCutcheon on 14th March 1891 and their second daughter, Annie Roberta, was born in Garvagh on 24th October 1893. Annie served with the VAD from 20th September 1917 until 21st March 1919 at military hospitals in Basingstoke, Stockport and Herne Bay in Kent.

County Monaghan

The war memorial for St Salvator's Church of Ireland is located in front of the church in the Castle Leslie Estate at Glaslough, County Monaghan. The church is also referred to as Glaslough (Donagh) Parish Church. It is a freestanding war memorial, erected around 1930, comprising a limestone shaft, with a frieze at the top in which '1914 1918' is inscribed in high relief. The shaft is topped with a projecting support for a sculpted figure of a lion. The memorial was unveiled by Colonel Sir John Leslie and dedicated by the Right Reverend Dr Day, Bishop of Clogher, on Sunday 27th February 1921.

The memorial records the names of nine men from the parish who died in the Great War and includes details that are not normally present on memorials (e.g. death date, type of death, location of death).

Named on the memorial are three sons of Samuel Steenson and Sarah Steenson (nee Hearst) from the Corraghmaxwell townland:

- **Samuel Steenson**, 2nd Battalion Royal Irish Fusiliers, was 26 when he was killed in action on 13th May 1915 and is commemorated on the Ypres (Menin Gate) Memorial in Belgium;
- **Thomas Steenson**, 21st Battalion Canadian Infantry, was 20 when he was killed in action between 15th and 18th August 1917 and is commemorated on the Vimy Memorial in France; and
- **Robert Steenson**, 16th Battalion Cameronians (Scottish Rifles), was 24 when he died of wounds in 3rd Scottish General Hospital in Glasgow on 16th May 1918 and is buried in Glaslough Church of Ireland New Cemetery.

County Tyrone

The **County Tyrone War Memorial** is situated at the junction of Bridge Street and Drumragh Avenue in Omagh, but does not fall neatly into any of the classifications detailed in the Introduction. Newspaper reports at the unveiling of the monument describe it as, *a massive obelisk of hammered granite* whilst it is classified as a cenotaph on the Imperial War Museum's UK War Memorials website.

The memorial, designed by Richard Francis Caulfield Orpen of Dublin, features a dedicatory panel engraved in limestone at the base and, above it, a bronze relief panel designed by Rosamund Praeger, which features an angel hovering above two dead or dying soldiers – the angel is holding a tribute of laurel leaves with the words "From Tyrone". The construction contract was handled by Purdy and Millard of Belfast (who were the contractors for several district memorials in County Tyrone) and the monument was unveiled by the Governor of Northern Ireland, James Albert Edward, the Duke of Abercorn on 28th September 1927.

In January 1919, Dungannon Rural Council adopted a resolution commending to the people of the district a proposal to erect a public memorial in Dungannon in honour of the soldiers who had fallen in the war. A committee was appointed to act in the matter, and it was decided to request the Urban Council to nominate representatives to act with the Rural Council Committee. In June of the same year, the Dungannon Urban District Council approved plans for the erection of a public war memorial in Market Square, *to consist of a bronze figure of soldier mounted on a raised pedestal*. The **Dungannon War Memorial** is approximately 18 feet and 6 inches in height and features the figure (approximately 8 feet 6 inches in height) of a sergeant holding a grounded rifle in his left hand and a standard or flag in his right hand, the pole being topped with a laurel wreath to symbolise victory. The statue, designed by Frederick William Pomeroy of London, stands on a sandstone plinth which rests on a granite base. The memorial was constructed by R Patton & Sons of Belfast.

At the front of the base is a bronze dedicatory panel surrounded with a laurel wreath and bearing the inscription:

IN MEMORY OF THE SOLDIERS AND NURSES WHO GAVE THEIR LIVES
FOR FREEDOM AND HUMANITY IN THE GREAT WAR.
1914–1918

The plinth has four bronze panels listing the fatalities from Dungannon – two panels record the names of the fallen from the Royal Inniskilling Fusiliers and one records the fallen from other regiments and Dominion Forces. A fourth panel is entitled **Additional Names of our Soldiers** and records the names of men identified as fatalities of the Great War after the erection and dedication of the memorial. Panels for the fatalities of the Second World War were added to the base of the monument.

The memorial was unveiled by Lady Ranfurly on Saturday 11th November 1922 and, during the unveiling ceremony, Brigadier General Ricardo's speech included the following words:

> *Let the comradeship of the trenches, where no division of creed or class was known, be with them to the end. The memorial should remind them of their duty to ex-Service men, especially the scarred and maimed in mind or body, many of whom to-day were unemployed. The men whom they honoured were all volunteers. No compulsion was needed to urge them. They lived and died free men.*

The **Moy War Memorial** is situated in the village square, facing St James'  Church of Ireland, and is constructed from Sicilian marble. It features a soldier in full battledress uniform with a bugle at his lips, playing the Last Post. The front face of the plinth is engraved with the names of the 36 men who made the supreme sacrifice. Below the names of the fallen are these words of King George V, *The men of Ulster on many fields, have proved how*

nobly they fight and die. The other three faces are engraved with the names of 174 men who served, with the names of 10 women who served being recorded after those of the men. The monument was made by Purdy & Millard of College Square North in Belfast, but the name of the designer is not known, although there is a clue at the base of the statue.

The memorial was unveiled on 11th November 1924 by the Honourable Mrs Philip Nelson Ward, sister of Viscount Charlemont, as Viscountess Charlemont was unable to be present due to the death of her father. After the memorial had been unveiled, Major Williamson read the names of the fallen and, as he called out each name, a comrade replied, "Killed in action, Sir" or "Died of wounds, Sir", as appropriate.

Archibald Small Aird, a retired Tea Planter, and Frances Frances Aird (nee Kimmitt) of Jasmine Lodge, Charlemont had five children, three of whom served in the Great War and are commemorated on the Moy War Memorial. **Archibald Thomas Aird** (born 25th May 1898) enlisted with the Royal Irish Fusiliers and, whilst undergoing training at Newtownards, was sent for officer training, being commissioned on 26th June 1917. Second Lieutenant Aird was serving with 18th (London Irish Rifles) Battalion, London Regiment, when he was killed in action on 30th November 1917 and has no known grave, being commemorated on the Cambrai Memorial  in Louverval. **Gilbert Aird** (born 15th January 1887) and **Elizabeth Margaret (Bessie) Aird** (born 4th May 1888) both survived the war.

Another war memorial in Ulster to feature a bugler is the tablet commemorating the fallen from Orange Lodges 359 and 461 and Royal Black Preceptory 130 – the memorial, which also features a bar of music, was unveiled in Downpatrick Orange Hall in May 1920 and is now on display in the Somme Museum in Conlig.

The **Castlederg War Memorial** is located in a park bounded by Main Street, John Street and The Diamond in the centre of the town. The original memorial erected in around 1938/1939 was a 25-foot high rectangular clock tower with three illuminated dials.

Original War Memorial (Courtesy of James A Emery BEM)

In August 1940, the *Ulster Herald* reported that the clock on Castlederg War Memorial had been stopped for four months and it was still not functioning in December 1948. In 1951, the *Ulster Herald* reported that the three clock-faces on the Castlederg War Memorial displayed different times.

In 1995, the original memorial was replaced by a rectangular column with the upper portion engraved with poppies.

In November 2001, as a result of research by James A Emery BEM, a new memorial tablet was dedicated which included additional names for both world wars.

They Played The Game

Unlike many other sports, the Irish Football Association and leading association football clubs did not erect war memorials or monuments. In recent years, some association football clubs – notably Linfield and Distillery – have erected memorial tablets.

At least eleven golf clubs have memorial tablets or rolls of honour naming members who served or died in the Great War, as do the Royal North of Ireland Yacht Club at Cultra and the County Antrim Yacht Club in Whitehead.

The new gates and grounds for the **Cregagh Athletic Club** were dedicated as a war memorial on Saturday 30th June 1923

In April 1919, a public meeting was held at Knock Methodist Lecture Hall to inaugurate a scheme to commemorate the members of **Knock Rugby Football Club** who had fallen in the Great War.

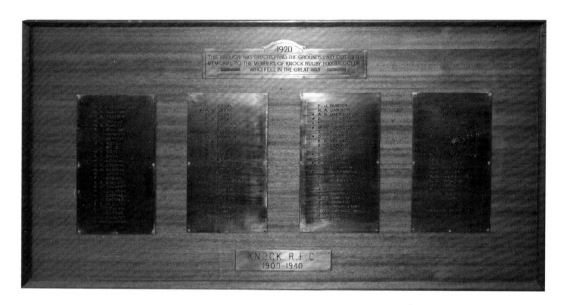

The club's former pavilion had been sold when matches had been suspended for the duration of the war and £65 from the sale funds was to be used to produce a tablet listing the names of the fallen. Captain Herbert Dixon MP, who was chairing the meeting, reported that they desired to raise funds to buy enough land for two pitches and a pavilion. Debentures were sold at the meeting, the first (£50) being bought by William McCalla, with over £660 raised on that evening. The new grounds and pavilion located at Hawthornden Road in Belfast were officially opened by Captain Herbert Dixon MP on Saturday 9th October 1920. The Roll of Honour contained four brass panels, listing the names of the 103 members who served, and identifying the names of the 28 members who died. It was attached to an oak tablet that also bore the club crest in colour. The pavilion, designed by John Seeds, took the form of a bungalow with fine dressing and bathrooms and tiers of seats capable of accommodating over 100 spectators. The inaugural match at the new grounds was against North, who won by two tries to nil. One of the players on the Knock team was **Frederick William Zebedee** who served in the ranks with the North Irish Horse before receiving a commission with the Royal Irish Fusiliers on 24th September 1918. He had been educated as a boarder at the Masonic Boys' School at Dundrum in Dublin and is commemorated on the Roll of Honour for Townsend Street Presbyterian Church in Belfast. The club ceased activities during the Second World War and did not recommence after that war. The brass panels from the Roll of Honour (but not the club crest) were later attached to a new tablet, which has a brass plaque engraved with "Knock RFC 1900–1940". The tablet is held at the Headquarters of the Ulster Branch of the Irish Rugby Football Union.

The **North of Ireland Cricket and Football Club** erected a memorial tablet listing the men from the club who had died for King and Country – 253 members served, with 60 being killed and 30 receiving gallantry awards. The oak memorial, engraved with the club's monogram, was made by Purdy & Millard and was unveiled on Wednesday 18th May 1921 by the Marquis of Londonderry at the club's pavilion on Shaftesbury Avenue in Belfast. The memorial is now located in the Board Room at the Northern Ireland War Memorial in Talbot Street, Belfast.

Cliftonville Cricket and Lawn Tennis Club erected a tablet listing the names of one woman and fourteen men from the club who died during war service. The memorial tablet was placed in the club's pavilion at the cricket ground, located at the junction of the Cliftonville Road and Oldpark Avenue, and was unveiled by Lieutenant Colonel Arthur Brownlow Mitchell on Monday 28th March 1927. In 1972, the club was forced to vacate the ground after a series of sectarian attacks against members and the looting and burning of the clubhouse by a hostile mob. It is assumed that the memorial was destroyed in the fire.

In some sports, the governing authorities elected to have war memorial trophies. The **Irish Amateur Swimming Association (Ulster District)** introduced a war memorial shield in 1921 for which club squadron sextets compete at an annual gala - a team from the Wellington Club in

Belfast Telegraph, 30/11/1920

Belfast won the inaugural gala. The competitions were held at a number of locations in Belfast, including Templemore Avenue Baths, the Belfast Waterworks and the Grove Baths. The gala is now held at the Bangor Aurora Complex each November on the Saturday preceding Remembrance Sunday. In 2017, the trophy was won by Bangor Swimming Club.

The **Cross-Country Association of Ireland (Northern Branch)** instituted a Northern War Memorial Trophy for which Junior teams competed over a six-mile course. The inaugural competition was held at Belvoir Park on 27th February 1920 and the trophy was won by the Willowfield Temperance Harriers (79 points)

with Duncairn Harriers (82 points) a close second and City of Belfast (120 points) a distant third. In 1921, the trophy was won by Duncairn Harriers with Willowfield coming fifth. In 2017, the trophy was won by the Finn Valley Athletic Club from County Donegal.

The Ulster Branch of the Irish Rugby Football Union erected a unique memorial at the entrance to its rugby ground at Ravenhill. The **Ulster Rugby Memorial** was described as, *a piece of architectural excellence unsurpassed for beauty of design and execution by any other similar memorial throughout the country.* (*Northern Whig*, 23rd January 1926)

The " Last Post," which was sounded by buglers of the 1st Battn. The Durham Light Infantry.   ("*Northern Whig*" Photograph.)
Northern Whig, 23/01/1926

The original memorial arch was designed by Belfast jeweller Sharman D Neill and erected under the company's supervision. It was unveiled by Mr T J Strain, President of the Irish Rugby Football Union, on Friday 22nd January 1926. Monsieur Morel, Assistant Secretary of the French Rugby Union, laid a wreath at the memorial. On the following day, the Ireland rugby team defeated the French team by 11 points to nil in a match that was described in the *Belfast News-Letter* as, *one of the poorest displays of Rugby football ever witnessed in a representative game.*

The 1936 Annual Meeting (as recorded in *Belfast News-Letter* on 23rd September 1936), reported that the War Memorial at Ravenhill was unstable and the committee had authorised a complete renovation.

Praeger Memorials

The Holywood artist and sculptor **Sophia Rosamund Praeger** designed several war memorials in Ulster, mainly in connection with Non-Subscribing Presbyterian Church congregations, but also for two Belfast schools, a shipyard and a county.

The memorial in **First Holywood (Non-Subscribing) Presbyterian Church** is relatively plain, featuring a young girl and a young boy holding out flowers, symbolising the thankfulness of future generations for the sacrifices made in the Great War. The memorial in **First Presbyterian Church (Rosemary Street, Belfast)** was dedicated on 26th February 1922 and its imagery is traditional. The central portion features a figure from the classical period holding a standard, with a dedicatory panel to the left of the figure. There are battle scenes depicted below the dedicatory panel and the panel listing the names of the six fatalities. The memorial in **All Souls Non-Subscribing Presbyterian Church** on Elmwood Avenue in Belfast was dedicated on 6th November 1921 and features allegorical imagery. There is a figure of a pilgrim holding a staff and treading on a snake whilst viewing a far-off castle that is set on a hill and accessed by a steep, winding path. There are sandbags at the start of the path and rays of light are shining behind the castle. Below the names panel are the words **I Press On**. The crushing of the snake (representing evil) allows humankind to focus on a better and more secure future which requires effort to achieve.

Rosamund Praeger executed the sculptures for the gothic-inspired **Campbell College War Memorial**, made of Runcorn stone, which was unveiled by General Sir Alexander Godley on 7th April 1923. The memorial was designed by Captain James Reid Young (of the Young & Mackenzie firm of architects) who had served with the Army Service Corps. In February 1920, the *Belfast Telegraph* published an artist's impressions of the war memorials planned for Campbell College. There was to be a memorial tablet erected in the Central Hall and a sixteen-foot high Celtic Cross in the quadrangle. The Celtic Cross was never erected and the 1923 memorial tablet featured some differences to the 1920 design, mainly in the statuary.

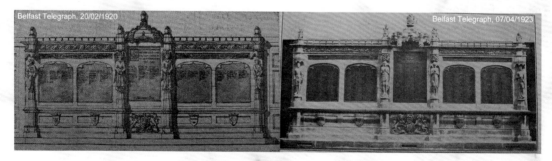

The central portion of the memorial features a brass panel embossed with a representation of St George slaying the dragon and lists those who died. Above the panel is a stylised Maltese cross. The central portion is surmounted by an elaborate battlemented cornice, the carving of which includes crowns and boars' heads, topped with an engraving of the school crest. The central portion is flanked by statues of two male angels, one is holding a laurel wreath ("Life") and the other an inverted sword ("Death"). The Royal Coat of Arms is engraved in the stone below the central portion.

There are a further four brass panels, two to either side of the central panel, listing those who served. Above these panels is a tracery featuring the national flowers of the United Kingdom. The outer edges of the memorial feature another two statues, one of a medieval soldier holding a shield ("Courage") and the other of a medieval herald holding a trumpet ("Endeavour"). Along the top of the memorial are four griffins holding armorial shields representing England, Ireland, Scotland and Wales. Along the bottom of the memorial are shields representing the four provinces of Ireland (in a different order to the 1920 artist's impression).

The architect firm of Young & Mackenzie was also responsible for the general design of the **Belfast Royal Academy War Memorial**, which was constructed in Portland stone. Three Belfast companies were involved in the production of the memorial. James Edgar Winter carried out the construction work whilst the school crest was emblazoned by George Morrow & Son and the bronze tablet was cast by Musgrave & Company. Rosamund Praeger executed the sculptures of the two angels, with heads bowed and holding inverted swords, which flank the panel on which the names of the dead are recorded. Immediately above the commemorative panel is a stylised Maltese cross, identical in shape to the one on the Campbell College memorial. The first name on the war memorial is VAD Nurse Winifred Elizabeth du Mesney Atkinson, who is mentioned in the Female Fatalities chapter. The memorial was unveiled on Thursday 13th May 1921 by the Right Honourable Reverend Thomas Hamilton, Vice-Chancellor of Queen's University Belfast.

Rosamund Praeger also executed the sculptured pieces on the **Workman Clark War Memorial**, which was originally situated in a prominent corner position on the right-hand side of the main entrance to the company's head office. The memorial, which takes the form of a tryptich, was unveiled by Sir Edward Carson on Friday 8th August 1919. The central panel features a medallion carved with a profile of Lieutenant Edward Workman MC and a biography is engraved below the medallion. The lower portion of the central panel records the names of five other officers who died, and the two side panels record the names of 20 Non-Commissioned Officers and 97 privates who fell. Above the three panels, the following was engraved in the stonework:

Eternal Honour give / hail - and farewell - / to those who died in that full splendour / of heroic pride / that we might live.

At the top of the memorial, there was a three-panel pictorial frieze showing men working at aspects of shipbuilding, men marching off to war and a battlefield scene featuring the burial of a man. It is not known what happened to the full memorial after the company's demise in the late 1920s. However, the three panels were attached to the outer wall of the Pump House in the Titanic Quarter and rededicated on Friday 16th May 2008 by the First Minister for Northern Ireland, the Reverend Doctor Ian Paisley MP.

Hidden Memorials

The purpose of this section is to highlight memorials that are not generally accessible to the public, although most can be accessed by requesting permission.

The overwhelming majority of war memorials and rolls of honour in Ulster are located in churches but many schools also have memorials. Similarly, there are memorials and rolls of honour in the halls of many fraternal societies. Several commercial and public service organisations also have war memorials or rolls of honour on their premises.

The war memorials for the **Ulster Reform Club**, the **Union Club** and the **Ulster Club** are all located in the former's premises on Royal Avenue in Belfast. As this is a private club, access must be arranged by a member of the Ulster Reform Club (URC). In the 1920s, the URC had funded the erection of a YMCA Red Triangle club on the corner of the Shankill Road and Spier's Place in Belfast. The club was officially opened by Sir James Craig MP on 1st November 1924 and the dedication plaque reads, *in grateful recognition of the services rendered by the men of the Shankill district in the Great War 1914-1919*. When this YMCA Club was closed, the plaque was returned to the Ulster Reform Club and is on display in its premises.

In Belfast City Hall, the memorial windows commemorating the **North Irish Horse** in both world wars are located in the main entrance on the ground floor and are accessible to the public. However, memorials located in the rotunda on the first floor are not generally accessible and include the **36th (Ulster) Division** memorial window, the **Belfast Corporation Employees** memorial and the **Belfast Corporation Gas Department Employees** memorial. A parchment Roll of Honour recording the names of Belfast Corporation employees who served in the Great War hangs in the Council Chamber.

The **Midland Railway Company (Northern Counties Committee)** memorial takes the form of an obelisk with the names of the fallen and those who served recorded on the faces of the plinth. The memorial was erected in the Midland Railway station at York Road and was unveiled by Major General Sir Oliver Nugent on 24th November 1921. The memorial is now located in the NIR Translink Depot on York Road. The memorial tablets for the **Great Northern Railway** and the **Belfast & County Down Railway** are on public display in the concourse at Central Station in Belfast.

The parchment Rolls of Honour for both world wars for the **Ulster Steamship Company** (Gustavus Heyn and Company, also known as the Head Line) are located at the premises of Heyn Group at Corry Place in Belfast.

The parchment Rolls of Honour for both world wars for the **Belfast Harbour Board** are on display in the foyer of the Belfast Harbour Commissioners Office in Corporation Square in Belfast.

The war memorial window for **St John's (Laganbank) Church of Ireland** was moved into storage at St Anne's Cathedral when the congregation re-located to Orangefield in the 1930s.

The Rolls of Honour for the **Balmoral Industrial School** and **McCrea Magee College** are held in the archives at the Public Records Office for Northern Ireland, the references are CR1/69/R/2 and NUU/5/1/2 respectively.

As has been referred to in the Preface, the war memorials and rolls of honour for the **Belfast Banking Company** and the **Northern Banking Company** are on display in the Northern Bank's Head Office in Donegall Square West in Belfast.

Missing Memorials

Whilst many war memorials in Belfast, particularly those in churches, were destroyed during the German air raids in 1941, others have been lost for other reasons (e.g. the memorial in Albert Street Presbyterian Church was destroyed in a fire in the early 1970s). The fate of other memorials is not known and some of these are detailed in this section.

In March 1918, the **Ulsterville Harriers** endowed a Memorial Bed in the UVF Limbless Hospital in memory of clubmates who had died during the Great War. Trooper Roland (Rollo) Curlis, 3rd Battalion Australian Light Horse, was killed in action on 19th May 1915, aged 39. He is buried in the Shrapnel Valley Cemetery on the Gallipoli Peninsula in Turkey and is commemorated on the **Newtownbreda Presbyterian Church War Memorial**. Roland Curlis was born on 3rd January 1876 at Holmes Street in Belfast to Thomas and Jane Curlis. He married Harriet Clarke on 31st May 1898 in Fountainville Presbyterian Church in Belfast. Roland was employed as a plumber when he enlisted on 24th August 1914 at Morphettville in South Australia.

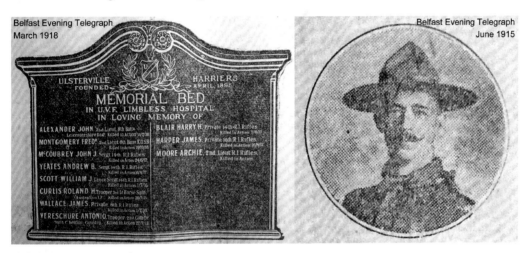

Belfast Evening Telegraph March 1918

Belfast Evening Telegraph June 1915

In April 1919, a memorial tablet commemorating the war fatalities from the **10th Belfast Boy Scouts Troop** was presented to the Ulster Hospital for Women and Children on Templemore

Avenue by Mrs McMordie, President of the Troop. The scouts of the troop had raised £74 to endow a cradle above which the tablet would be mounted. Rifleman George William Paysden MM, 14th Battalion Royal Irish Rifles, died of wounds at No. 2 Casualty Clearing Station on 11th October 1916, aged 22, and is buried in the Bailleul Communal Cemetery Extension at Nord in France. George Paysden was born in Ballymacarrett on 16th May 1894 to James Thomas and Jessie Margaret Paysden. In December 1916, the *London Gazette* reported that George Paysden had been awarded the Military Medal, probably for an act of gallantry during the advance on 1st July 1916.

In October 1920, the **Belfast Co-Operative Society** erected an eleven-foot high memorial in the main entrance to its York Street store in Belfast. The memorial had three sections. The lower section had a panel with the dedication, *In memory of those who fell; in honour of those who served.* The middle section had brass tablets set in oak panels on three of the faces – the tablet on the front face listed the twelve employees who died, whilst the tablets on the other faces listed the sixty-eight employees who had served. The column is topped with a dome on which stands a winged figure, holding a flaming torch and laurel wreath. One of the fatalities listed on the memorial was Private Charles Elder, North Irish Horse, who was killed in action on 7th November 1918, aged 25. He is buried in Dourlers Communal Cemetery Extension in France and commemorated on the **Castleton Presbyterian Church War Memorial**. Charles Elder was born on 22nd May 1893 at Parkmount Street in Belfast to James and Annie Elder.

In February 1922, the **Ulster Amateur Flute Band** erected a war memorial in its band-room on Downing Street in the Shankill area of Belfast. The memorial, which takes the form of a tablet

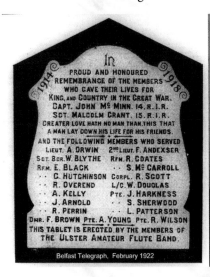

Belfast Telegraph, February 1922

Belfast Evening Telegraph, January 1917

of Sicilian marble mounted on black slate, was the work of Samuel Livingstone of Beverley Street. The names of two band members who had died, and nineteen members who had served during the war were engraved on the memorial, which was unveiled by the Reverend W J Dunlop, Rector of St Stephen's Church, Millfield. Lance Sergeant Malcom Grant, 15th Battalion Royal Irish Rifles (attached to 107th Trench Mortar Battery), was killed in action on 3rd January 1917, aged 35. He is buried in the Ration Farm (La Plus Douve) Annexe cemetery at Hainaut

in Belgium and is commemorated on the **St Michael's Parish Church War Memorial**. Malcolm Grant was born on 23rd February 1880 at North Queen Place to James and Margaret Grant. He married Mary McCartney on 25 December 1909 at St Anne's Parish Church in Belfast and they had three children. Before the war Malcolm Grant worked at Queen's Island and had been a member of the North Belfast Regiment UVF and the Dunmurry Drumming Club.

Other memorials or rolls of honour whose locations have not been identified are:

- Belfast Post Office War Memorial (Tablet, November 1925)
- Dunville & Company Roll of Honour (Parchment, March 1921)
- Glen Printing & Finishing Company (Newtownards) Roll of Honour (Parchment, December 1917)
- Inglis Bakery Memorial (Tablet, April 1919)
- Malone Training School War Memorial (Tablet, July 1920)
- Manor Street YMCA Roll of Honour (Parchment, June 1920)
- North East Bar War Memorial (Tablet, March 1920)
- Willowfield Unionist Club War Memorial (Tablet, November 1923)